PLEASURE HORSES

BY
JEROLYN ANN NENTL

EDITED BY
DR. HOWARD SCHROEDER
Professor In Reading and Language Arts
Dept. of Elementary Education
Mankato State University

DESIGNED & PRODUCED BY
BAKER STREET PRODUCTIONS
MANKATO, MINNESOTA

COVER GRAPHICS BY
BOB WILLIAMS

CRESTWOOD HOUSE
Mankato, Minnesota

PERRY ELEMENTARY LIBRARY

LIBRARY OF CONGRESS CATALOGING IN PUBLICATION DATA

Nentl, Jerolyn Ann.
  Pleasure horses.

  (Horses, pasture to paddock)
  SUMMARY: Discusses the pleasure and responsibility of owning and riding a horse and provides information about different breeds, riding techniques, equipment and feeding, housing, and grooming a horse.
  1. Horses--Juvenile literature. 2. Horsemanship--Juvenile literature. (1. Horses. 2. Horsemanship.) I. Schroeder, Howard. II. Title. III. Series.
SF302.N46   1983   636.1   83-7823
ISBN 0-89686-228-3

International Standard Book Numbers:	Library of Congress Catalog Card Number:
Library Binding 0-89686-228-3	83-7823

PHOTOGRAPH CREDITS

Cappy Jackson: Cover, 19, 41, 43
Cindy McIntyre: 5, 10, 24, 25, 33
Wide World Photos: 7
Bob Williams: 11, 17
Lynn Rogers: 9
Patti Mack: 12, 13, 28, 36
University of Minn. Technical College: 15, 34
Alix Coleman: 23
Peter R. Hornby: 29, 31, 38, 45

CRESTWOOD HOUSE

Hwy. 66 South, Box 3427
Mankato, MN 56002-3427

Copyright© 1983 by Crestwood House, Inc. All rights reserved. No part of this book may be reproduced in any form without written permission from the publisher, except for brief passages included in a review. Printed in the United States of America.

TABLE
OF
CONTENTS

Introduction 4
1. The Pleasure Horse 6
    Wild Horses
    The Modern Horse
    Breeds, Colors and Markings
    Conformation
    Who Should Own a Horse?
2. How to Handle & Ride a Horse . .16
    Tack
    Handling a Horse
    Learning to Ride
    Riding Styles & Gaits
    Aids and Clothes
3. How to Care for a Horse 28
    Pasture or Stable
    Feeding a Horse
    Grooming
    Keeping a Horse Healthy
4. How to Have Fun with Horses . .38
    Clubs, Gymkhanas & Rodeos
    Showing, Jumping and Dressage
    Breeding & Training
5. The Old Horse 34
Glossary 46

INTRODUCTION

Vicky sat down on a bale of hay and took off her hat. The sun was already bright and she was hot and sweaty. She took a deep breath and decided to relax for a few minutes before feeding Sunshine her grain.

Sunshine was Vicky's horse. As Vicky watched Sunshine munching on some hay she smiled and felt a rush of warm feelings. In the five years that Vicky had owned Sunshine, they had become close friends and steady companions. They had worked hard learning how to move gracefully together. Now when they went for a ride, they could both relax and enjoy each other.

Vicky did not mind all the hard work it took each day to care for Sunshine. She did not even mind getting out of bed at five in the morning any more. Vicky laughed a little to herself. Before she owned a horse, she used to like to sleep late almost every morning. Now she looked forward to seeing the sun's first rays light up her bedroom.

She would get up, get dressed, and eat her breakfast. It did not take her long to get to the stable. After grooming Sunshine and cleaning out her stall, they would be off for an hour-long ride. Then there was just enough time to cool Sunshine down and feed and water her before Vicky had to leave for school.

It had become Vicky's favorite time of day.

① THE PLEASURE HORSE

There are about seven million pleasure horses today. They are owned and ridden by young and old people, healthy and handicapped people. Both men and women like to go horseback riding.

Those who love horses know that having one of their own is something special. Horses are big and powerful, sleek and graceful. Learning to ride a horse is a challenge. Owning one is a big responsibility.

WILD HORSES

The history of wild horses goes back thousands of years. This ancient horse was much smaller than today's horse — about the size of a fox. It had four toes on each forefoot and three on each hindfoot. As the centuries passed, the horse grew bigger and stronger. Its toes grew smaller. Finally, each foot had only one middle toe. This was surrounded by bone to protect it. It had become a hoof.

Many small herds of wild horses roamed the world, looking for grasslands on which to graze. As these horses began to settle into different parts of the world, their size and shape changed. How each kind developed depended on the weather and food where they lived. Some grew to be huge and heavy, with

These wild horses, at a zoo in England, are from outer Mongolia.

calm natures. They became the work horses of the world. Others stayed lighter and became very fast and high-spirited. These lighter horses became the riding horses of today.

THE MODERN HORSE

The horse is a big animal, compared to the ancient wild horse. An average horse might weigh 1,200 pounds (544 kg) and stand fifteen hands high. A hand is a unit of measurement used by horsemen. One hand equals four inches (10.3 cm), which is the

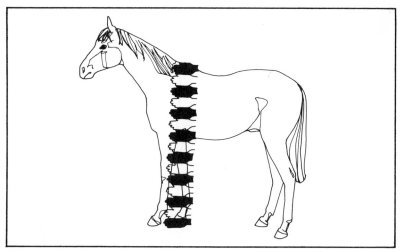

A horse's height is always measured from the withers to the ground by using the width of an adult hand.

average width of an adult's hand. A horse's height is always measured at the withers. This is the highest point of the horse's back, between its shoulder blades. Horses under fourteen-and-a-half hands high are called ponies. Those sixteen-and-a-half hands and taller are called heavy horses. These are the horses that work in harness. Horses that are fourteen-and-a-half to sixteen-and-a-half hands tall are called light horses. These are the riding and racing horses.

BREEDS, COLORS AND MARKINGS

There are many different breeds of horses today. Most racing horses are thoroughbreds. Riding horses are usually a mixture of breeds rather than any one pure breed. This does not mean that they are not good animals. Many are very beautiful, well-built horses, but their line of ancestors is not known. They are called pleasure horses, or stock horses.

Pleasure horses come in shapes, sizes and colors of all kinds. They also have many different head, leg and body markings.

A horse's coat may be all one color — like black, light gray, brown, or chestnut (chestnut is a reddish color). There is also a yellow-gray color called dun. Some horses are a mixture of colors. If a horse is called a bay, it is a shade of brown but its mane and tail are black. Sometimes bays also have black lower legs. Horses with golden colored coats of yellow-

A little child is becoming friends with two bay horses.

brown, are called palominos. Their manes and tails are blond or silver. Sometimes palominos also have white lower legs. A roan is a horse whose coat is a solid color but white hairs grow throughout it. A horse whose coat has two or more colors in patches is called a pinto or paint.

Markings give many varieties to a horse's looks. A narrow white mark up and down the center of a horse's face is called a stripe. A small white mark on its forehead is called a star. Such a mark on its nostril is called a snip. A horse with a blaze face has a white muzzle up to a point between its eyes. White foot markings that extend up the leg from the hoof are called socks, boots, or stockings.

The mare shows a stripe face while her foal has a star on its face.

CONFORMATION

All these colors and markings make some riding horses better looking than others. But the most important thing is how a horse is built — its bones, body shape, and muscles. This is what horsemen call conformation. A horse with good conformation looks "just right."

All horses share certain rules of good conformation. The hindquarters is the most important region. This is the horse's source of power. The hips and thighs should be firm, with good muscles. The legs should be strong. They should be well under the horse so that they can support its weight properly. A horse's feet must be large enough to support it. But they must not be so large that they cause the horse to stumble.

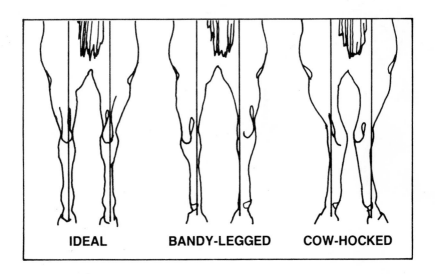

IDEAL   BANDY-LEGGED   COW-HOCKED

The neck should be well-muscled so that it can support the head. It must not be too long or too thick. The head should be nicely shaped. It is important that a horse's nostrils be large and flared, so it can breathe easily. The eyes should be large, wide open, and clear — if they are not, the horse may be sick or old.

A horse's back should be smooth, with firm muscles. Its belly must not be pulled up, which is another sign of sickness. A horse's chest should be strong and firm — not too narrow or too wide. Likewise,it's best if a horse's back is not too long or too short.

Exactly what good conformation is varies from breed to breed. Conformation also varies according to what type of riding a horse will be used for. It is

difficult to learn how to judge good conformation. The best teacher is experience with many different kinds of horses over a long period of time.

WHO SHOULD OWN A HORSE?

Many people admire horses from afar. Their beauty and power are the things of which dreams are made. Some people will try to make their dreams come true. They will get close to a horse by visiting someone who keeps horses in a stable or pasture. That ends the dream for some of them. Once up close, they fear the power of this animal that is so much bigger than they!

Those for whom this first touch is a pleasure, will try to put their dreams into action. No longer do they want to admire horses. They want to ride and become friends with them. They also want to learn how to care for them.

There are many different ways a person can do this. People can rent, lease, share, or own a horse. There are many different rights and responsibilities that go with each. Which way people choose will depend on several things — their age, the amount of money they have to spend, and where they live. Most important of all, it will depend on how much time and effort they are willing to put toward a horse.

Many riding stables, in both the city and the country, rent horses. Some also lease them. Renting a horse means paying by the hour to ride it. The stable owners and their helpers take care of the horse. A person who rents a horse from a stable may not always get to ride the same horse each time. This is why some people lease horses. Leasing means paying a set amount of money each month for a certain amount of riding time on one special horse. The horse belongs to the stable owner, but the person who is leasing it helps care for it. Sharing a horse is also becoming very popular. Sharing means two or more people go together to buy, care for, and ride a horse.

Owning a horse is not easy. It takes lots of space and quite a bit of time and money. A pleasure horse may cost $500 to $1,000. Proper care may cost several hundred dollars more each month. An owner must also have the proper place to keep a horse and be willing to spend at least an hour each day with the animal. Anyone that can't manage all these things should not try to own a horse.

A neglected horse gets bored and unhappy. Such horses may get sick.They may become difficult to ride, too.

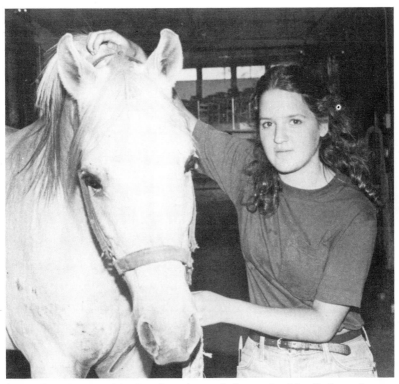

Spending time and caring for a horse is important for its happiness.

②
HOW TO
HANDLE AND RIDE
A HORSE

Almost anyone can get on a horse's back and ride. A good rider can do much more than that.

A true expert is one who knows how to control all types of horses in all kinds of situations. To do this a person must first learn about horses as animals. They must also understand how to use all the pieces of horse equipment, called tack. Skilled riders know that there is always more to be learned. Knowledge and skill come only after many years of being around horses.

To learn to ride correctly, most people choose to take regular lessons. They may also get a job at a stable to learn how to care for a horse. Many stables have riding schools. Some private horse owners also give lessons. People who want to become good riders will choose teachers carefully. They will search for someone who is a good rider as well as a good teacher. They will make sure that the teacher's horses are healthy and trained well. A good riding school doesn't have to be fancy, but the stables, pastures and riding areas should be clean.

TACK

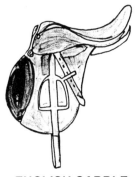 

ENGLISH SADDLE   **WESTERN SADDLE**

There are two general types of saddles used today — English and Western. The English saddle is lighter and flatter than the Western saddle. Its flaps are set forward and often has knee rolls to help support the rider during a jump. The Western saddle has a higher pommel, or front, and a higher cantle, or back. It also has a horn on the pommel. The Western saddle is sometimes called a stock, or cowboy, saddle. It is the saddle used by cowboys and ranch hands to do their work. The Western saddle has rings, leather strings, and straps to carry the tools of that trade. The Western saddle flaps are set back to help protect the cowboy's legs. Both English and Western saddles are made of leather. English saddles are used with a saddle pad. Western saddles are used with a saddle blanket. There are two main reasons for using the pads and blankets. The first is to help keep hair and sweat from the horse off the saddle. The second reason is to keep the saddle from rubbing the horse's back.

A saddle must fit the horse properly and be comfortable for the rider. Both types of saddles come in different shapes and sizes, depending on the type of riding being done and the size of the horse.

Attached to the saddle are the stirrups. These are used as footrests while getting on and off the horse and while riding. Stirrups on all types of English saddles are made of metal. Those on Western saddles are made of wood and may be covered with leather.

The bridle fits over a horse's head. There are many different kinds of bridles. The type that is used depends on what the rider wants a horse to do. All bridles have three main parts, however — the headpiece, the bit, and the reins. The headpiece is the part that holds the bridle on a horse's head. The bit is the metal piece that fits in a horse's mouth. The reins are the leather straps connected to the bit. A rider uses the reins to put pressure on the bit. The pressure is what controls and directs the horse. English-style reins are about five feet long and closed at the ends. Western style reins may be as long as eight feet, either open or closed at the ends. Some bridles and bits use a double set of reins. This gives a rider even more control of a horse. It takes much more skill to use double reins.

The bridle fits over the horse's head and includes the headpiece, the bit, and the reins.

A special type of bridle is called a hackamore. The hackamore is a bridle without a bit. It puts pressure on the horse's nose and chin when the rider uses the reins. This pressure controls and directs a horse in the same way as pressure on a bit does. Usually a hackamore is used only for training a young horse, before using a bridle with a bit.

The halter is the simplest tack item. It is a bridle without a bit and reins. Halters are used to lead and tie a horse. Generally, a rope is attached by a clip to a ring on the halter beneath the horse's chin.

HANDLING A HORSE

Before a horse can be ridden, it must be properly bridled and saddled. That sounds easy, but most beginners have a very difficult time learning how to do it!

The horse is always approached on the left side, called the near side. It helps to speak calmly to the horse, calling it by name, and perhaps stroking its neck. Approaching a horse from the front may make it back away. Coming up from the rear may get the beginning rider a swift kick! It's best to approach a horse in the area of its front left leg.

Anyone bridling a horse should be especially careful of its eyes and ears. Bridling a horse takes patience and a gentle touch. Roughly forcing a bit into its mouth will only scare the horse and will make it harder to bridle the next time. The saddle should also be gently placed on the horse's back.

LEARNING TO RIDE

The first thing to learn about riding a horse is how to get on and off. This is called mounting and dismounting.

A horse is always mounted and dismounted from the near side. To mount an English saddle, the rider faces the horse's tail. With a Western saddle, the rider faces the horse's head. The reins are always held in the left hand. The left hand is placed on the horse's withers. The right hand may grip the pommel. The left foot is placed in the stirrup. As the rider springs upward, the right leg swings over the rear of the horse. The right foot is then placed in the stirrup on the far side.

A well-trained horse will stand still for its rider to mount and dismount. Skilled riders are careful not to poke a toe into the horse's belly or to land on its back with a bump.

RIDING STYLES

Once in the saddle, riders must learn to balance themselves. They must also learn how to use the reins and their legs. There are different ways to do all these things. They are called the riding styles, or seats.

For pleasure riding on a English saddle, riders sit erect in the middle of the saddle with their bodies slightly forward. Their shoulders are back and their backs slightly arched. One rein is held in each hand, with the arms forming a straight line from elbow to bit. The stirrups are adjusted so that the leg is slightly bent.

On a Western saddle, the rider also sits erect, but deep in the saddle and back against the cantle. The stirrups are longer so that the legs are almost straight. Both reins are held in the left hand, with the right hand at rest. Western-style riders must hold the reins higher, to clear the horn on the saddle.

Skilled riders control and direct their horses with very gentle signals of the hands on the reins. The horse's mouth, which holds the bit, is very sensitive. Pulling on the reins too roughly can "spoil" its mouth. Such rough handling can cause a horse to lose feeling in its mouth. Before long, the horse will be hard to control.

Skilled riders also use firm but gentle leg pressure to control and direct their horses. To get a horse to move forward, they press their legs against the horse's sides. They also press their weight into the saddle. As the horse moves forward, the riders allow their hands to move slightly forward. This loosens the reins, and is called "giving with the hands."

GAITS

The natural movements of a horse are called gaits. The three basic ones are the walk, trot, and canter. A fourth gait is the gallop, but it really is only a faster canter.

Pleasure riding on an English saddle.

A skilled rider's position in the saddle changes with every gait. At a walk, the rider sits erect in the saddle but swings gently from side to side in rhythm with the swaying movement of the horse. At a trot, the horse does not sway from side to side, so the rider does not sway either. This time the rider moves up and down slightly. There are two ways to ride the trot — sitting in the saddle or rising slightly in the stirrups. These are called sitting the trot or posting the trot. When posting, the rider leans forward off the saddle each time one pair of the horse's legs hits the ground.

At a canter, the rider sits upright in the saddle. Only the upper part of the rider's body moves in rhythm with the horse. At a gallop, the rider leans forward out of the saddle and moves with the horse.

In a walk the rider sits relaxed and erect.

A rider gets the feel of a horse's gaits only through practice.

Skilled riders signal their horses to advance from one gait to the next by easing the reins and gently pressing their lower legs against the horse's flanks. Turning is also done with slight signals from the rider. Shifting the weight of the body in the saddle helps signal a turn. Western-style riders also use neck, or indirect, reining. They pull the reins across the neck of the horse on the side opposite of the way they want their horse to go. English-style riders use direct reining. They pull slightly on the rein on the side to which they want the horse to turn, and then give with the other rein.

To stop, skilled riders do not yank on the reins. They simply steady them, stopping any forward

At a gallop the rider leans forward and moves with the horse.

PERRY ELEMENTARY LIBRARY

movement of their hands. This causes the horse to feel the bit. Since no horse likes the feel of a bit, it slows down and stops. Riders also signal a horse to stop by pressing their weight back into the cantle of the saddle.

To get a horse to back up, a rider pulls on the reins gently and applies the same kind of leg pressure used to urge the horse forward. This causes the horse to feel the bit, just as it did when stopping. But the leg pressure tells the horse to move backwards.

These movements are very basic. There are many variations to each of them. Learning the basics well is the first step toward becoming a skilled rider. To correct mistakes, beginning riders should always have an expert with them when they practice. Bad habits are very difficult to break once they're started!

Beginning riders may first practice on a longe. The longe is a rope attached to the horse's bridle that is held by a teacher. It usually is about thirty feet long. Rider and horse walk, trot or canter in a circle around the teacher. Later, riders practice in straight lines and in other patterns on their own. This is called schooling.

Beginners should have three goals: to strengthen their muscles, to gain a firm and balanced seat in the saddle, and to learn a gentle touch with the reins. At the same time, a rider should try to build trust and respect with the horse.

AIDS AND CLOTHES

There are many aids to help a rider control and direct a horse. The riders voice, hands, and legs are the most important. But there are other things, too. These are called unnatural, or artificial, aids. Spurs and whips (English-style riders call them crops) are two of the most common. Such aids are always used with only the lightest, gentlest touch! Good riders never hurt their horses.

The clothes a rider wears depends on the type of riding to be done and the weather. For pleasure riding, a person might wear comfortable pants and shirt, plus a pair of boots. The boots should have heels, but no buckles to catch on things. A jacket may be needed in colder weather, and rain gear in wet weather. While learning, it is a good idea to wear a riding hard hat. Many riding schools and stables require them.

Advanced riders like to have a certain look that fits their style of riding. English-style riders prefer breeches or jodhpurs that are narrow at the knee. They wear formal riding coats, dress boots and perhaps a derby or a top hat. Western-style riders like tapered jeans, cotton shirts, cowboy hats and Western boots.

③
HOW TO CARE
FOR A HORSE

Caring for a horse can draw rider and horse closer together. They will be more comfortable with each other when they are out for a ride.

All horses need food, water, and a place to live. They also need someone to groom their coats and look after their health. When horses ran wild, they did all this for themselves or they died. Since mankind has domesticated, or tamed, the horse, these things must be done for it.

A good scrub-down will keep the horse's coat healthy.

PASTURE OR STABLE?

Home for a horse can be either a pasture or a stable. A pasture is a more natural home. A horse that lives in a pasture can eat, drink and run as much as it wants, just as its wild ancestors did. If it has other horses for company, that is even better. The pasture must be fenced and have plenty of grass. Horse owners also need to be sure that there are no plants growing in the pasture that are poisonous to horses . Foxglove, ragwort, and nightshade are just a few of these deadly plants.

There must be plenty of water available. If there is no pond or stream to provide fresh water, there must

A pasture can provide the exercise and food needed for the horse.

29

be a water trough, or container, that is never dry. There should also be some kind of shelter, so a horse can get out of the wind or rain.

Horses that are kept in a stable should each have their own stall. These are separate places where each horse can feed and rest by itself. The walls of each stall usually go only part way up to the ceiling. This allows light and fresh air throughout the stable. It also lets each horse feel the company of the other horses. The stall should have its own window for added light. This also lets a horse see outside. Some stables keep their horses in long, narrow straight stalls that are about five feet by twelve feet. Others use box stalls that are at least ten feet square. Each stall must have a feed rack, or box, and a supply of fresh water. A stable should have an outside exercise area, too. This is called the paddock.

It is very important to keep a stable clean. The daily chore of mucking out, or cleaning, each stall may seem unpleasant, but it is necessary. Stalls that are not cleaned daily can quickly give a stable a bad odor. They will attract a lot of flies that bother the horses. A dirty stall can cause the horse that lives in it to get sick.

Straw is the most common bedding for horses kept in a stable. It should be changed every morning and loosened up at night.

Horses living "out" can get plenty of exercise by running around the pasture. Those kept in a stable must be exercised daily for at least half an hour. Twice daily is best. Weekend rides are not enough exercise for a horse kept in a stable. If there is no time for a ride, a horse should be turned out into the paddock for a run. A horse that does not get exercise is soon bored. It may begin to weave back and forth in its stall or kick at the walls. It may bite its blankets or eat its straw bedding. The horse may soon become sick.

Horses that live in a pasture don't need to be exercised.

FEEDING A HORSE

A horse is a big animal, but its stomach is quite small. Because of this, a horse likes to eat small amounts quite often. A horse that is living out in a pasture that has plenty of grass and fresh water can eat and drink as it wants. Most often it will nibble small amounts of grass throughout the day. A horse that is kept in a stall must be fed and watered. This is usually done at least twice a day, morning and evening. Three times a day is better.

Grass is a horse's natural food. Horses living "out" can be fed hay in winter if there is not enough grass growing. Stabled horses are fed hay all year. Hay is really dried grass. Sometimes people confuse hay with straw. Straw is the dried stalks of grain that are left after the kernels of grain have been harvested. It is only used for bedding.

Horses are also fed grain. Oats, corn and barley are the grains used most often. Sometimes they are sweetened with a small amount of molasses. A horse also needs salt in its diet. A block of salt should always be left where a horse can lick it.

A horse's health depends on what it is fed — and how much. A horse that is not fed or watered properly may become ill. Too much feed or water at the wrong time can also harm a horse. Exactly how much a horse is fed and watered depends on its size, age, and the amount of exercise it is getting. Each horse will require different amounts.

If horses live in a pasture, they don't need hay or grain.

Feed and water racks must always be kept very clean. Feed that is spoiled or dirty can make a horse sick.

GROOMING

Taking proper care of the outside of a horse is very important. The care of the horse's hairy coat is called grooming. It helps keep the horse clean and healthy. Daily grooming is a must for stabled horses. Horses kept out in a pasture do not need to be groomed as often. They need the oil that builds up on their coats to help protect them from the weather.

Grooming takes special tools. A rubber curry-comb removes mud, loose hairs, and dandruff. The dandy brush, with its stiff bristles, gets out the dirt. A softer, body brush gets off the oil. A metal curry-comb is used to remove hair and dirt from the brushes. A cloth, called a stable rubber, is used to smooth and shine the horse's coat. A damp cloth or sponge is used to clean around a horse's eyes and nostrils. A small, very soft brush is used on its face, below its knees and on any other area that might be sensitive. A flat metal comb is used for the mane and tail.

Anyone grooming a horse should use a firm, but gentle touch. A horse's skin is so sensitive it can feel a fly on its back!

The most important part of grooming is caring for

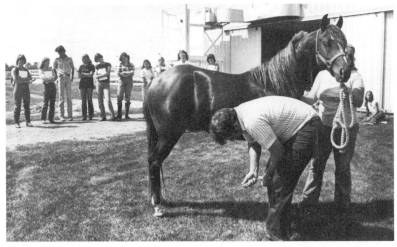

Students learning to care for a horse are shown hoof care.

the feet. Each foot must be cleaned daily with a hoof pick to get out any dirt or stones. Some people also oil each hoof to keep them from becoming brittle and cracking.

Horses that are ridden on hard surfaces such as roads need "shoes" on each hoof. A horseshoe is a piece of metal in the shape of a "U" that is nailed to the bottom of the hoof. The shoe helps protect the hoof and keeps it from wearing down too quickly. It does not hurt the horse to nail the shoe onto the hoof. A horse has no feeling in its hoofs. A hoof is really thick bone, like a toenail.

Shoeing is done by farriers. Their job is to remove each horseshoe, trim the hoof, and reset the shoe. A horse's hoof grows about one-quarter inch each month, so this job is done every six weeks, or so. As a rule, shoes can be reset two or three times before they are worn out.

KEEPING A HORSE HEALTHY

Healthy horses have shiny coats, bright eyes, and good appetites. They are alert and full of energy. When given the chance, they will run as much as they can.

Any horse that does not look or act this way may be sick. Horses that are restless and sweaty, that do

A horse that likes to run is probably healthy.

not want to eat, or that lack energy may be sick. Those that limp or flinch when they are touched may be injured. A good veterinarian, or animal doctor, can help find the cause and the cure.

Horses need to be dewormed about once a year. It

is also wise to have them vaccinated against disease.

Colic and thrush are two common kinds of horse sickness. Colic is really a stomachache, but it can be very serious. A horse can die of colic if it is not treated quickly. Colic can be caused by eating too much or by eating spoiled food. Riding a horse right after feeding it, or giving it too much water too quickly after riding it, can also cause colic. Thrush is a disease of the feet. A horse infected with thrush will have very tender feet and may become lame. There will also be a very bad odor around the feet. Thrush should not occur if a horse's feet are cared for daily and its stall is kept clean.

Injuries are far more common in horses than illness. These, too, can be prevented. No sharp objects or edges should be allowed around a stable or pasture. No horse should be ridden too hard or too long. No horse should be asked to do something for which it is not prepared. Following such rules will help prevent strains, sprains, cuts, and bruises. Slight injuries can be handled in the stable with a first aid kit. More serious ones should be turned over to the veterinarian as soon as possible.

Any illness or injury that is allowed to go on too long may cause permanent damage to a horse. It is better to call the veterinarian too soon than too late. Smart horse owners and stable managers call a vet whom they like and trust before they ever have a serious problem.

④
HOW TO HAVE FUN
WITH HORSES

Once a person has learned how to ride and care for a horse, there are many things that can be done on horseback. Most people today ride simply for pleasure. Going for such rides is called hacking. The horse used, no matter what breed it is, is called a hack. Some families even take hacking vacations. A long, slow ride across the countryside is a great way to spend a bright, sunny day. The trails may be across rolling hills, up a forested mountain or along a sandy beach at the water's edge. Open spaces give riders a chance to feel the freedom of an all-out gallop.

People and horses out for pleasure riding is called "hacking."

CLUBS, GYMKHANAS, AND RODEOS

Riders often join clubs of different kinds. Club members have a chance to learn more about horses and improve their riding skills while having fun with each other. The Pony Club of America and the 4-H Club are two popular ones. Some riders also choose to join humane groups which help prevent the abuse of horses.

Many riding clubs hold special meets called gymkhanas. These are fun contests of riding skill. There may be short and long-distance races, water and sack races, or egg-and-spoon contests. All are meant to improve the riders' seat and the control and direction of their horses.

Horse clubs are often asked to be in parades.

For some riders, fun and games are not enough. They want to enter serious competitions. The Western-style rider may choose rodeos. These contests began a century ago when the cowboys of the West drove cattle to market each year. When the long drive was finished, they got together to show off the skills of their trade. Today, rodeos are held all across North America. Riding bucking horses is one of the main events. Only the most skilled riders can stay on a bucking horse.

SHOWING, JUMPING AND DRESSAGE

English-style riders like showing, jumping, and dressage contests. These can be very formal events.

The goal of showing is to display the horse's conformation, movements, and training. It also displays the rider's skill. Horses are shown at different gaits. If the rider leads the horse it is called showing in-hand. If the rider is mounted it is called showing under saddle.

Riders may jump their horses over one high fence or a number of shorter ones all in a row. They may even jump side-by-side.

Dressage is advanced "schooling." Circles, lines, and figure-eights are done at various gaits and speeds. These exercises are called "figures." The most advanced kind of dressage riding is called Grand Prix. Very few people ever attain this kind of perfect understanding between rider and horse, because it takes many years of training.

Skilled riders may also go on to fox hunting, playing polo, or driving. When a horse is put into harness and directed from behind, it is called driving. The driver rides in a cart, carriage, or buggy that is harnessed to the horse.

This rider performs dressage "figures."

BREEDING

Breeding is an interest that may turn into a lifetime hobby or business.

A female horse, or mare, is bred with a male horse, or stallion. Generally, there is only one baby born each year. It is called a foal. Sometimes there may be twins, but this does not happen often. Male foals are called colts. A female foal is called a filly. While still very young, colts that are not going to be used for breeding are castrated. This is called gelding. A gelding is much easier to handle and ride than a stallion. Most colts are castrated — only about ten percent are used for breeding.

Raising the foal of a pleasure horse can be enjoyable and rewarding. Most people raise them so they have more horses to ride. Some raise them to sell. Usually breeders raise only foals of a certain breed of horse for showing and selling.

TRAINING

Breaking and training a foal takes patience, understanding, and a lot of experience with horses. Once again, a gentle touch and a soothing voice are a must. Breaking a horse means introducing it to the halter, bridle, and saddle for the first time. Foals will be ready to halterbreak when they are several months old. Most pleasure horses are not broken to bit and saddle until about the age of three. Then their real training to accept a rider can begin.

Most pleasure horses are not ridden until they are about four years old. Horses are at their best from about five to ten years of age. Most stay in top form until the age of fifteen, if they are given good daily care.

Mother and foal enjoying time together.

⑤
THE OLD HORSE

Some horses may live to be forty years old. However, most live only to the age of twenty-five. They are seldom fit for riding after they get into their late teens.

An old horse will lose weight and muscle tone. The shine will leave its coat. A horse's digestive system and its teeth change with age, too. Eating may become a problem.

The kindest thing to do for these old friends is to turn them loose in a good pasture. They should not be forgotten, however. Retired horses need a good supply of food and fresh water, just as they did when they were younger. They still need to be groomed, and their feet and teeth need regular care.

Most of all, retired horses need company. A horse is a living, feeling animal. They miss the people they served. People who love horses will take time to visit their retired friends. A few soothing words, some pats on the neck and maybe a treat do not take long. Most old horses like to be taken on a walk around the pasture, too.

The time will come when an old horse dies, however. People who have cared well for their horses should have no regrets. They will have happy memories to live with forever!

GLOSSARY

BIT - The metal piece placed in the horse's mouth by which a rider controls and directs the horse.

BREED - A certain kind of horse.

BRIDLE - The headpiece, bit, and reins used to control a horse.

COLIC - A horse illness; a stomachache.

COLT - A young male horse, less than four years old.

CONFORMATION - The bone structure and body shape of a horse.

FARRIER - One who cares for a horse's hoofs.

FILLY - A young female horse, less than four years old.

FOAL - A baby horse.

GAIT - The natural movements of a horse — walk, trot, canter, and gallop.

GELDING - A castrated male horse.

HACKAMORE - A bridle that has no bit.

HAND - A unit of measurement used to describe a horse's height; one hand equals four inches.

HOOF - A thick bone that surrounds the front and sides of the toe on each foot of a horse.

HORSESHOE - The U-shaped metal piece that is nailed to a horse's hoof.

LONGE - A long rope fastened to a horse's halter or bridle that is held by a teacher to train a horse or teach a rider.

MARE - A mature female horse.

PADDOCK - A small enclosed area where horses can be exercised and trained.

POINTS - The different parts of a horse's body.

REINS - The leather straps that are held by the rider to control and direct a horse.

SEAT - A rider's position in the saddle.

STALL - An enclosed place in a stable where one horse is kept.

STALLION - A mature male horse.

STIRRUP - The footrests attached to a saddle.

TACK - Horse equipment.

THRUSH - A disease of the feet in horses.

THE HORSES
PASTURE TO PADDOCK

**READ & ENJOY
THE ENTIRE SERIES:**

**RUFFIAN
THE PONIES
THOROUGHBREDS
HUNTERS & JUMPERS
PLEASURE HORSES
HARNESS RACING
RODEO HORSES
DRAFT HORSES**

CRESTWOOD HOUSE

636.1
Nen

636.1   Nentl, Jerolyn Ann.
Nen
          Pleasure horses.

565757   09882B